Adolf Eichmann
Engineer of Death

Ruth Sachs

THE ROSEN PUBLISHING GROUP, INC.
NEW YORK

To my father (of blessed memory) and mother, who taught me to pay attention to how people speak, to see the soul in another's eyes lest I ignore truth or believe a lie. To Finley Shapiro, who listened as I worked through the confusing and often contradictory messages of the Eichmann saga, a sounding board par excellence.

Published in 2001 by The Rosen Publishing Group, Inc.
29 East 21st Street, New York, NY 10010

First Edition

Library of Congress Cataloging-in-Publication Data

Sachs, Ruth.
Adolf Eichmann: engineer of death / by Ruth Sachs. —
   1st ed.
       p. cm.
Includes bibliographical references and index.
ISBN 0-8239-3308-3 (alk. paper)
1. Eichmann, Adolf, 1906–1962.   2. Holocaust, Jewish (1939–1945). 3. Nazis—Biography. 4. War crime trials—Jerusalem. 5. World War, 1939–1945—Atrocities. I. Title.
DD247.E5 S18 2000
364.15'1'092—dc21

00-010632

Manufactured in the United States of America

Contents

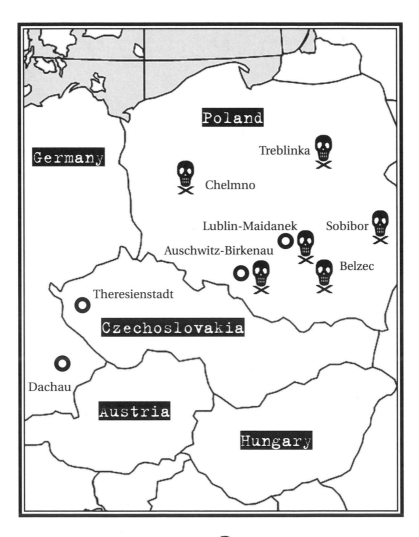

Poland

Germany

Treblinka

Chelmno

Lublin-Maidanek   Sobibor

Auschwitz-Birkenau

Belzec

Theresienstadt

Czechoslovakia

Dachau

Austria

Hungary

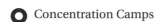 Concentration Camps   Extermination Camps

Introduction

"Accused, the court convicts you of crimes against the Jewish people, crimes against humanity, a war crime, and membership in hostile organizations." With these blunt words, Judge Moshe Landau, speaking before a stunned audience shortly after 9 AM on December 11, 1961, passed final judgment on the career and accomplishments of Adolf Eichmann.

The verdict itself came as no surprise to anyone in the courtroom. Indeed, if the three judges had acquitted Eichmann, the police would have had difficulty keeping peace among the spectators. The pale man in the bulletproof glass cage had angered so many people that everyone expected the judges to find him guilty.

Eichmann's attorney, Dr. Robert Servatius, along with most news reporters in the room, thought that Judge Landau would add suspense to the reading of the verdict. Dr. Servatius had raised a few troubling legal questions. He denied Israel's right to try his client. He argued over witnesses he could not call. He tried to portray Eichmann as a mere administrator who did not know what he was doing.

When Judge Landau immediately declared Eichmann guilty, the spectators grew silent, shocked at the bluntness of the judge's words. Eichmann, who had stood at Judge Landau's orders, sat down heavily. Only then did the judges read the entire judgment against Eichmann. Judge Landau went first, describing in general the atrocities that Eichmann had committed. He said that Eichmann's deeds would be remembered until the end of time.

The second judge, Benyamin Halevi, continued reading, responding to the challenges Dr. Servatius had made to the court. Judge Halevi had researched every

Adolf Eichmann told the court that he was a guilty
accomplice in the slaughter of six million Jews.

question and found that there was adequate
precedent for an Israeli court to try Eichmann.
The third judge, Itzhak Raveh, then directed
his comments to Eichmann's crimes. There
was no doubt in the eyes of the court about
Adolf Eichmann's guilt. It took the judges two
full days to read the whole judgment against
Eichmann. The television cameras rolled, and
reporters filed their stories.

Eichmann sat in his glass cage, surrounded by policemen, staring at the judges and the menorah behind them as if he were not interested in anything being said. He wore a dark suit, and every once in a while rubbed his eyes as if he were tired or bored. With his thick glasses and pasty face, he looked more like someone who worked in a post office or bank. And that was exactly the problem the reporters had when they wrote their stories for newspapers and magazines across the world. They had come to Jerusalem expecting to find Frankenstein or Count Dracula. Instead they found a quiet, unassuming bureaucrat, or so it appeared.

On this Monday, however, December 11, 1961, the judges told the world that yes, they had read all the facts, and the facts said that he was guilty of unimaginable crimes.

1. An Unhappy Youth

On March 19, 1906, Karl Adolf Otto Eichmann was born in Solingen, Germany. Solingen is in the Ruhr district, not far from Cologne. The city is famous for specialty knives and other items made of high-quality steel. It is a region of industry.

The Eichmanns left Solingen when Adolf was still in elementary school. The family moved to Linz, Austria, where Adolf's father became the business director for the Linz Trolley and Electricity Corporation. When Eichmann later described Linz, he used almost poetic words. He spoke of the Inn Valley, which was heavy with wheat. He recalled with obvious pleasure the beauty of the "pearl" of nearby Traun Lake, a town called Gmunden,

Eichmann had happy memories of
his childhood in Austria.

close to the cliffs of Traunstein, which he termed the sentinel of the Alps.

Eichmann said that his childhood was glorious. He remembered mountain climbing and sitting in coffeehouses with his friends. Days, he noted, of love, leisure, and life. He told the story of begging flowers from a certain Mr. Bugele for his girlfriend when he was young. Yet people who knew him told a different story. Adolf's mother died when he was a small boy. His father remarried. Some claim that Adolf was a slow learner. Others assume that he had difficulty with his stepmother. But of the seven children in the Eichmann family, Adolf, the oldest, was the only one who did not graduate from high school.

Adolf resented being an outsider as well. His parents were Lutherans and remained in that church even after moving to all-Catholic Austria. With no separation of church and state, religion was a mandatory subject in German and Austrian public schools. If a family allowed their children to miss

religious instruction, they were branded
outcasts. But if the Eichmann children took
the courses, they found their own faith
subject to ridicule.

Not only did Adolf's family remain
Lutheran, but they attended church regularly,
too. It is therefore not surprising, and probably
one of the few truthful things Eichmann ever
said about his childhood, that a Jewish child
named Harry Selbar was his best friend in
school. But Adolf hated it when classmates
taunted him about his "Jewish" appearance.
His dark features pained him. "The little Jew,"
his schoolmates would tease him. He found
nothing funny in their mocking.

Economic Collapse

In the early 1920s, the German economy
crashed. Germany and Austria found
themselves trying to pay war reparations with
money they did not have. These reparations
were detailed in the Treaty of Versailles, which

After the German economy crashed in the 1920s, unemployment was common.

marked the end of World War I. The winning countries, France and England, declared that Germany had to pay the cost of fighting the war. When Germany could not pay, it started printing money as briskly as possible. Economists were not fooled by this scheme and adjusted the exchange rate as fast as Germany printed new money. Before long, people were taking a wheelbarrow of deutsche marks to the store to buy a single loaf of bread. Prices in stores changed hourly. When a company tried to pay its employees, the money it took out of the bank in the morning often could not cover even a single person's wages by lunchtime. People told tales of going into a restaurant to eat

During the economic collapse of the 1920s, Germans carried money to the bank in wicker laundry baskets.

dinner and not being able to pay for a cup of coffee an hour later. They found it cheaper to use money as wallpaper, since paper money could not buy wallpaper. This period of hyperinflation made money worthless and wiped out people's savings.

Adolf's father tried to put him through a technical school for engineers when his son dropped out of high school, but Adolf completed only two semesters. With the widespread economic crisis, it appeared for a time as though the young Eichmann would be a complete failure and an embarrassment to his solidly middle-class and well-respected family. When the senior Eichmann left his job at the trolley company to start his own mining business, he put his unlucky child to work for him. Adolf started at the bottom in his father's mining enterprise, as a common laborer and miner. Since class distinctions still meant something in Austria in the 1920s, his father eventually got Adolf a position as a sales clerk at the Upper Austrian Elektrobau Company.

Eichmann's reaction to this job was typical. Whenever he was bored, he lost interest in what he was doing. And being a sales clerk, tied to a desk, definitely bored him. He yearned for action. Once again, his family pulled strings for him. His stepmother was related by marriage to a wealthy Jewish family in Czechoslovakia. She convinced her cousin to act as a go-between for her stepson. At his trial in 1961, Adolf proudly stated that the Vacuum Oil Company had offered him a contract as a traveling salesman, enabling him to leave behind his boring desk job. He neglected to mention that a certain Mr. Weiss, general director of that American-based company, and a Jew, had been the one to extend such a generous offer to an unqualified young man.

In 1932, the Vacuum Oil Company transferred Eichmann to a desk job in Salzburg. Where he had had a large region at his command before, he was again chained to a single place. His unhappiness grew. He saw himself stifled in a dead-end job and began to distance himself from the company. In an attempt to break out of his doldrums, Eichmann considered joining a club of sophisticated men called Schlaraffia. This lodge was made up of middle and upper middle-class businessmen who simply wanted to get together to have a good time. They practiced refined humor and believed their purpose in life was to cultivate merriment and happiness.

Ernst Kaltenbrunner, the son of one of Adolf's father's friends, heard about Adolf's interest in this comic group. Ernst, a serious and successful attorney, tried to talk him out of such nonsense. Kaltenbrunner offered Adolf the choice between the "merry society" and the organization he himself had joined: the National Socialist Party. When Eichmann insisted that he could join both, Kaltenbrunner reminded him that the Schlaraffia lodge was a branch of the Freemasons. The National Socialists, or Nazis, would not allow Freemasons to be members.

Ernst Kaltenbrunner, an early comrade of
Hitler's, is shown here at the Nuremberg trials.

Now Eichmann had to decide. Should he go after wealth and position and hobnob with these businessmen pranksters? Or should he link up with Kaltenbrunner and his Nazi gang? In the end, Adolf Eichmann did not have the luxury of choice. He was kicked out of Schlaraffia for a social blunder. He invited Franz Resl, a prominent writer and "chief cuckoo" of the group, out for a drink. As the most recent, youngest, and therefore lowest-ranking member, this was not his right. In 1961, Eichmann expressed no regrets for the way fate chose the Nazi Party for him. On the contrary, he used mythological words to describe how he viewed the National Socialists. They were gods. They performed heroic deeds. These gods were capable of manly death and fearless loyalty.

Eichmann and his new friends devoured the words of the Nazi newspaper, the *Völkischer Beobachter.* They heard fiery words about national disgrace, betrayal, and the dagger that had been thrust in the back of the German people by pacifists, communists, and Jews. The Nazi Party promised a restoration of the glory of the German army and vowed to "damn unemployment to hell." This was the party that would forever end the shame of losing the war.

"Lord God, how these words gripped us, stirred our blood," Adolf Eichmann told his interrogator in Jerusalem thirty years later.

Becoming a National Socialist

Adolf Eichmann officially joined the National Socialist Party on April 1, 1932. He was twenty-six years old and had a steady girlfriend named Veronika. He had found a way to tolerate the job in Salzburg—he simply left every Friday to spend the weekend with Veronika, traveling sometimes to Bohemia, other times to Linz; any place but Salzburg.

But Eichmann's old habits reappeared. He grew bored and tired of his job. He stated later that he was fired because of his membership in the Austrian Nazi Party. It may be true that in early 1933, after Hitler came to power in Germany, the Austrians temporarily outlawed the National Socialist Party, but it is unlikely that Eichmann's affiliation with the Nazis affected his job. His old friend Ernst Kaltenbrunner, for example, continued working in his father's law firm.

It is more likely that Eichmann was restless and needed some excitement in his life. He thought he could find that across the border in Germany. Eichmann packed his bags in July 1933 and headed for Bavaria. His new career in the exiled Austrian legion of the National Socialist army had begun.

2. Rising Through the Nazi Party

Eichmann joined the German army in a fit of enthusiasm, but once again, boredom swept over him before basic training was even completed. Whether at Lechfeld, or Dachau, the concentration camp, Eichmann hated his new life.

The life of a soldier did not suit Eichmann well. Always the same thing over and over again, day after day. The only bright spot in Private Eichmann's life was his first promotion. He had to prove himself in a so-called punishment drill. Not only did he complete it well, but he caught the attention of his superiors. Later he said that his success was due to his anger at his father for refusing to buy him gloves. He figured it would serve his father right if his hands froze off. Driven by his rage, he performed well.

At his trial in 1961, Eichmann claimed that he did not know that the views of the Nazi Party included anti-Semitism. He insisted that he joined for the adventure and because of the betrayal of Versailles. He repeated over and over that he did not hate Jews, that his crimes were not crimes against the Jewish people. They were not even crimes at all, but only the actions of a soldier doing what he was told to do. Eichmann was so firm about his lack of knowledge regarding the Nazi agenda that a few people at the trial were tempted to believe him.

Some reporters pointed to Eichmann's bad school record, as if to say, maybe he really did not read the signs and posters that singled out the Jews from the very beginning. Because he looked like a modern-day nerd, more than one person was willing to give him the benefit of the doubt. A prestigious reporter named Hannah Arendt, who covered the trial for *New*

Yorker magazine, spent two pages explaining how he could have been naive early on, with no criminal intent.

By now, Hitler had been in power for eighteen months. The Nazis had organized a boycott of all Jewish stores. All political parties except for the National Socialists had been banned. Plans were already under way to sterilize gypsies and other minorities. Anti-Jewish speechmaking increased. Jews were barred from civil service jobs and all teaching positions from preschool to university. Hitler preached publicly that Jews were subhuman. His platform included moves to deny German citizenship to all Jews, making them stateless and unprotected.

Eichmann was promoted from private to corporal in the Austrian Legion of the *Schutzstaffel*, or SS, who were Hitler's bodyguards. Then he volunteered for the *Sicherheitsdienst*, or the SD, the security service of the SS. Heinrich Himmler had founded the SD a year earlier. As Himmler's status grew within the Nazi Party, he handed over some of

Adolf Eichmann (*top left*) and an unidentified
Austrian SS man, Linz, 1931 or 1932.

his duties to men he could reasonably trust.
Reinhardt Heydrich, who had a career as a navy
spy, took over the SD, reporting directly to
Himmler. In the beginning, the SD was
supposed to collect information about other
Nazi Party members so that Himmler could
always blackmail his competitors. The unit
became so effective at this task that the SD
eventually became responsible for all

information gathering for the Nazis, including the Gestapo, the secret police.

At his trial in 1961, Eichmann complained that becoming a member of the SD had been a huge mistake. He said he had wanted to be one of the men that stood on the running boards of cars that carried important people. He had seen pictures of them in the newspaper. Even assuming he was telling the truth in 1961—that

SS Brigadeführer Reinhardt Heydrich is shown here at his desk in Gestapo headquarters.

he had confused the security service of the *Reichsführer* SS with the Reich security service that provided these bodyguards—he did not complain when the promotions started coming.

When Eichmann wrote about his early years in the SD, he filled page after page with trivial details about his breakfasts and his visits to barbershops, restaurants, bars, and coffeeshops. He complained about how inconvenient it was that he was not already married to Veronika because single officers had to bunk in barracks. After all this senseless detail, he finally described the job he was hired to do. Heydrich gave him a desk job—"enough to make my bones vomit," said Eichmann later. He reported to a "good-for-nothing" student who happened to be curator of the Freemasons Museum in Berlin. This museum, however, did not honor the Freemasons. Rather, it tried to show how terrible they were. Eichmann cataloged countless seals and medals from various Masonic lodges, what appeared to him to be a demeaning clerical task.

Now he came to understand why the Nazis hated the Freemasons. Among the Freemasons, Jews and Christians mingled freely, without distinction, with their peculiar oaths and rituals binding them together. "You could not tell a Jew from a Christian over their glass of wine," he pointed out in 1961. This was not meant as a compliment.

Eichmann asked to be transferred from his desk job cataloging Masonic artifacts to the new and special department that dealt with the "Jewish question." At his trial, he insisted that the department was originally conceived by an SS officer named von Mildenstein, who was a liberal, tolerant man who wanted to solve the "Jewish question" only on a political level. Despite the weight of the evidence against him, Eichmann expected the judges to believe that he followed von Mildenstein's example of treating Jews kindly, with greatest respect, and without the least bit of racism or religious persecution.

Ironically, the use of von Mildenstein as an example worked against Eichmann in his trial.

Eichmann maintained that once he joined the SD he had no choices, that everything was forced upon him and he could only obey or be killed. Yet the very man he identified as "first and greatest mentor and teacher" had quit the Jewish section and asked to be transferred to highway construction. Von Mildenstein was neither killed nor demoted.

Eichmann finally married Veronika and now qualified for more money and better positions. Before finalizing their engagement, which had been unofficial for several years, he requested a thorough check of her racial background to ensure that he was marrying someone who was totally Aryan. He did show a bit of a stubborn streak when it came to the actual ceremony. The Nazi Party expected him to have a civil wedding, with old German traditions replaced by new National Socialist symbols. But he chose to have a Lutheran wedding in Passau. However, when it became clear that his continued membership in the Lutheran church prevented additional promotions, he left the church without hesitation.

Eichmann enthusiastically took on the work of the Jewish section. Under von Mildenstein, he had been assigned to study Jewish orthodoxy. Before he left to work for Albert Speer's highway department, von Mildenstein convinced Eichmann to read Theodor Herzl's book, *Der Judenstaat* (The Jewish Nation), a Zionist, or Jewish, manifesto.

Adolf Eichmann had found his niche. Who else would read Zionist materials? The "Jewish question" filled a void and gave him something to do that no one else did. Eichmann tried to teach himself Hebrew and failed. He petitioned his superiors for tutoring, having found a rabbi who would be willing to work with him for the unbelievably generous sum of three marks an hour (a full dinner at a nice restaurant cost one and a half marks). While that request was denied, he did get permission to travel to Palestine to speak with Arab leaders about returning the Jews to that British-ruled country.

European Jews arrive in Palestine. The Nazis at first considered sending Jews to a homeland outside of Europe.

The Palestine trip turned into a fiasco, but Eichmann's report bolstered his reputation as the Nazi's "Jewish expert." He was able to pick up enough street Yiddish to fool his colleagues. Oddly, as the noose began to tighten for Germany's Jews after the Nuremberg Laws were passed in 1935 prohibiting marriages and other unions between Jews and non-Jews, Eichmann began to float rumors that he had been born in Palestine. He had gained just enough knowledge of Jewish affairs to be useful to his superiors. He professed admiration for the Zionists, whom he recognized as "nationalists" and "idealists" like himself. (Their goal of removing Jews to a homeland beyond Europe appealed to the Nazis at this stage as well.) Eichmann immersed himself deeply in Zionist philosophy. He sought to master Jewish customs and traditions. This knowledge became the weapon that he would later use against the Jews with deadly effect.

3. Freeing Austria of Jews

By 1938, Eichmann had achieved the rank of second lieutenant—not bad for someone who had not graduated from high school. His first really big break came along in March 1938, when Hitler annexed Austria. The days of the National Socialist Party being banned from Austria were long gone. German troops marched in unopposed and were welcomed with signs proclaiming the joy of Austrians at "coming home" to the Reich. The country no longer was called Austria. It had become the Ostmark, or "eastern frontier".

None of the world powers seriously challenged the military coup. A few American newspapers even saw the *Anschluss,* or annexation of Austria, as a positive development that would bring peace and stability to the region. A British travel guide from 1938 mentioned how delightful it was that travel between Germany and Austria had been made easier with the tearing down of the border between the two countries.

The Nazi takeover of Austria meant a significant upward move for Eichmann. Four days after the German military took over,

This poster in Vienna, hung after the *Anschluss*, reads, "Common Blood Belongs Together in One Reich!"

Eichmann arrived in Vienna. Suddenly, he was the official "Jewish expert," in charge of the Central Office for Jewish Emigration.

Hitler's ominous speeches and threats now became policy. Germany and Austria had to be cleared of all Jews. Since Hitler's notion of providing Germany with *Lebensraum,* or living space, had been known from the beginning, Eichmann knew that he had found a niche with room to grow. The more land Hitler conquered, the more Jews there were to expel.

Eichmann ordered all high-ranking and wealthy Jews released from the concentration camps where they had been imprisoned. At this point, the concentration camps had not yet been converted to extermination camps, but served as enormous prisons to "concentrate" Jews and political prisoners for labor pools. They were not pleasant places, but they had not yet become killing factories.

When the prominent Jews returned to Vienna, Eichmann invited them to his office to

calmly and rationally discuss the emigration
situation. The Jews criticized the emigration
system as it existed, pointing out that by the
time a person ran from one government office
to the next to obtain the proper permissions,
the original exit visa had already expired.
Eichmann listened attentively and appointed
these gentlemen as heads of Jewish councils.

Under Eichmann, Jewish institutions in
Vienna were reopened. Synagogues flourished
again briefly. One Jewish leader recalled at the
trial in Jerusalem that early in 1938, Eichmann
called him and his colleagues to his office. He
treated them as equals. They sat in his
presence, surprised at such civility from a Nazi
officer. His good mood did not last long. As
soon as he had the necessary information, he
turned it against the Viennese Jews.

Their complaints about the emigration
process were entirely justified, he advised
them. So he set up an assembly line. Anyone
wishing to leave Austria had to bring all of his
or her worldly possessions (or an inventory of

Jews were forced to wear the Star of
David and were expelled from their homes.

them) to the emigration board. They entered
the room with their assets and left with only
an exit visa and the small amount of currency
required by other countries to allow their
entrance. Eichmann's office took everything:
property, bank accounts, and apartments. All
in exchange for the privilege of leaving Austria.
If the Viennese Jews were not successful in
finding a foreign visa within the two weeks
allowed, they were sent to Dachau.

After Eichmann began to taste his success,
he became unrecognizable. Gone were his
polite mannerisms. He liked to keep the Jews
in his power guessing. One day he would be
thoughtful, allowing a Jewish congregation to
celebrate Yom Kippur. On the next day he
might slam his swagger stick on the desk and
threaten violence to the same people.
Around 100,000 Jews managed to leave
Austria safely, with nothing but their lives. It
did not take Eichmann and his staff long to
recognize the gold mine they possessed as
Jewish money and assets flowed directly to

his office with almost no accountability for the amounts received.

Hitler's main objective was simply to get rid of all the Jews in Germany and in the annexed or occupied territories. It was unimportant whether the Nazi officers involved made themselves rich off the Jews they deported. As long as the goal was kept in mind of ridding greater Germany of Jews, Eichmann and his staff knew there would be no reckoning regarding confiscated property.

When Eichmann's superiors heard of his success at moving Jews out of Austria, his assembly line methods were copied in Berlin and Prague. In Prague, his methods proved very effective. In less than six months, 35,000 Jews had been forced to leave, handing over all they owned before their ships sailed.

World War

In September 1939, Germany invaded Poland. Twenty-four hours later, Eichmann's office became one of the busiest and most important in the Nazi hierarchy. The number of Jews he had dealt with in Austria and Czechoslovakia now seemed ridiculously small. One hundred thousand Jews? There were more Jews than that in Warsaw alone. He had to figure out what to do with at least three million Jews.

Eichmann's office had already begun to experience problems finding nations that would accept the Jews he did not want. The United States and Britain put strict quotas on Jewish immigration. Eichmann found it harder to motivate people to give him everything they owned if they knew in advance they would not be able to enter another country. And now there was the war to worry about. After Germany invaded Poland, Britain and France declared war on Germany. Ships that were headed to America had to turn back or risk being sunk.

The Central Office for Jewish Emigration became a section of the Gestapo dealing with

Germany invaded Poland in
September 1939.

religious enemies of the state, specifically the Jews. After initial attempts at suppressing Freemasons and certain Catholic, Lutheran, and other religious groups, the National Socialists concentrated all their efforts on the Jews. Eichmann reported to Heinrich Müller, who reported to Reinhardt Heydrich, who reported directly to Heinrich Himmler, who reported to Hitler himself.

Hitler and Himmler were still thinking in terms of simply removing Jews from Germany. Despite provocative speeches, Hitler knew that he could not afford to draw the United States into the war at such an early date. The Nazis had to maintain a positive image while they made their long-term plans.

At the 1936 Olympics in Berlin, Hitler had gone to great lengths to paint a cheerful picture of the "Jewish question" in Germany. Jewish orchestras entertained international visitors. German orchestras played Mendelssohn, a Jewish composer who was otherwise banned. Hitler demonstrated to the world that Jews in Germany were separate but equal, making an unspoken comparison to the situation of African Americans in the United States.

Even three years later in 1939, Hitler's public strategy had not changed. Eichmann spent a full year attempting to devise a solution for moving millions of Jews out of Europe without killing them. His first idea had already failed. The British would not allow Jews to settle in Palestine. Eichmann continued to pursue this policy, meeting with Jewish Zionists already living in Palestine. The plan faced opposition not only from the British, but from the Arabs. The Grand Mufti of Jerusalem strongly supported Nazi goals for destroying all Jews and was not sympathetic to allowing millions of European Jews into the country.

Eichmann then tried a plan that had been discussed in Germany's foreign office before: emigration to Madagascar. He proposed to ship millions of Jews to this large island off East Africa and put them under the "protection" of Nazi overlords. In other words, he wanted to create the largest concentration camp ever known, with abundant slave labor at the Nazis' disposal. But Eichmann could never work past a gigantic problem. Germany was at war and needed all its ships for battle. Nothing could be released for other uses, even for such a "noble" cause as making Germany

Judenrein, free of Jews. The ships would be out on the open seas, sitting targets for Allied bombers and submarines.

The Madagascar plan was never put into action. Hitler changed the rules of the game before Eichmann could finish his proposal. Someone observed anonymously, "The year Eichmann wasted on the Madagascar scheme was the most harmless he ever spent."

4. A Humane Method of Killing

In June 1941, Germany invaded the Soviet Union, and the war was now to be fought on a grand and savage scale. The brutality of the black-uniformed SS increased dramatically. The boycotts of Jewish businesses, the robbing of Jews by forcing them to leave the country, the firing of Jews from government positions, the Nuremberg racial purity laws—suddenly these things appeared as nothing compared to the violence that now erupted. Even *Kristallnacht,* the night in November 1938 when every Jewish synagogue was burned to the ground and Jewish businesses were vandalized, felt like child's play to the Jews who still lived in Europe in the summer of 1941.

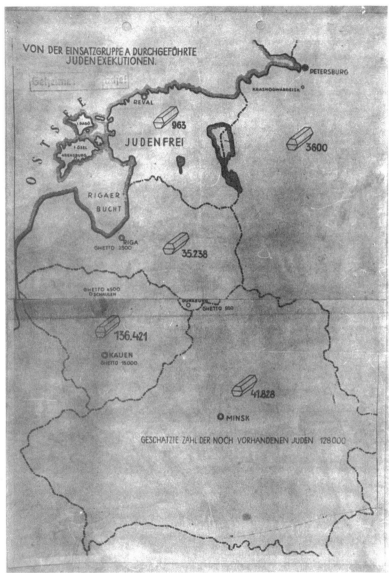

VON DER EINSATZGRUPPE A DURCHGEFÜHRTE JUDENEXEKUTIONEN.

Geheim

OSTSEE

REVAL

HAGO

ÖSEL
ARENSBURG

JUDENFREI

963

3600

PETERSBURG

KRASNOGWARDEISK

RIGAER

BUCHT

RIGA
GHETTO 2500

35.238

GHETTO 4500
SCHAULEN

DÜNABURG
GHETTO 950

136.421

KAUEN
GHETTO 15000

41.828

MINSK

GESCHÄTZTE ZAHL DER NOCH VORHANDENEN JUDEN 128000

This map accompanied a secret report on the mass murder of Jews by the *Einsatzgruppen*. The numbers of Jews executed are shown next to pictures of coffins.

As the German army swept across Poland and into the Soviet Union, special units of SS troops called *Einsatzgruppen* (literally, "operation groups") followed the regular soldiers. The only task of the *Einsatzgruppen* was to kill all who were deemed a security threat to the German Reich. The definition of "security threat" was purposely left vague. In one form or another, it included members of the aristocracy, professionals like lawyers and doctors, clergy, high-ranking politicians, and people who acted suspiciously. And, of course, every Jew was murdered, automatically put into the category of people who endangered the future of Germany. The killings incorporated the method Eichmann used with Jews during the forced emigration scheme, for after the *Einsatzgruppen* murdered the Jews in a town, the SS claimed everything they owned as property of the German government.

There were only four of these special troop units, each with its own murderous commander. On January 3, 1946, Otto

Ohlendorf, who was in charge of *Einsatzgruppen D*, described how his unit executed Jews:

> *We orally instructed our troops to liquidate, to kill, Jews and Communists. Men, women, and children. All Jews were brought to one area and told they were to be relocated. They were transported to the place of execution in a wagon so they did not know what was happening to them. They were shot, standing or kneeling, with no outer garments, and their bodies were buried in the trenches. Unit leaders had to make sure everyone was really dead. We took all their property, including clothes and watches.*

The four units kept track of how many Jews they killed. It became a kind of game to see who could kill the most, with Eichmann as the scorekeeper. All reports went through his office to be counted and added to a

Otto Ohlendorf, commanding officer of *Einsatzgruppen D*, from a trial photo.

commander's record. As the Germans started to lose the war a few years later, the Nazis tried to destroy these reports and almost succeeded.

Mass Murder

In less than a year, approximately 300,000 Jews had been shot and tossed into ditches.

Since the Jews in eastern Europe did not always wear the Star of David like the Jews in Germany and Austria, the SS executioners could not tell who was Jewish and who was not. That did not bother the SS. They decided they would shoot anyone who looked Jewish. By the end of the war, 1.4 million Jews had been murdered by the *Einsatzgruppen.*

Heinrich Himmler is shown here during an official visit to SS units in occupied Russia in 1941.

At his trial in 1961, when the prosecution questioned Eichmann about the activities of the *Einsatzgruppen*, he claimed that the murders had bothered him and that he went weak in the knees the one time he witnessed an actual execution. The prosecution reminded him of the many times he had made an attempt to be present when Germans killed Jews.

Eichmann had accompanied Heinrich Himmler to an execution in Minsk. The SS rounded up 400 Jews and killed them as a demonstration of their skills for their two bosses. Eyewitnesses said that Himmler, a fat and well-dressed general, nearly fainted, but Eichmann barely flinched. In fact, one of the Jews to be murdered was a young man with blond hair and blue eyes. Himmler thought he looked Aryan and tried to save him, but the machine guns had already started firing, and the young man was killed.

From there, Eichmann drove to Lvov, where the butchery had already taken place.

The bodies had been buried in a huge common grave with a thin layer of dirt spread over them. When Eichmann arrived, he said he saw blood spurting from the ground like geysers. That sight did bother him, he admitted later.

Himmler ordered that the SS find more "humane" ways for disposing of Jews. He was afraid of two things. First, as the war wore on,

This was one of the huge mass graves at the Bergen-Belsen concentration camp in Germany.

it would be harder and harder to find men who could pick up a rifle or machine gun and kill someone at close range. Second, since he believed Germany would win the war, he did not want the streets filled with ex-soldiers who could kill so easily. It might be bad for German society if the murders continued.

By now, everyone knew that the Madagascar plan, or any other plan that involved shipping Jews out of Europe, had been abandoned. Long before the words "Final Solution" became part of the Holocaust vocabulary, Himmler, Heydrich, Müller, and Eichmann knew that the only solution that counted was physical extermination.

Gas

One of the first alternatives used by the Germans had been tested years before. In the 1930s, "useless eaters" were euthanized by carbon monoxide poisoning. Useless eaters included people with incurable diseases or mental illnesses—people who would not be able to earn a living and would have to depend on their families or society for support. The Germans had emptied church-run orphanages and various clinics, most of which were located in small towns. There were a few protests, among them one from the bishop of Cologne, and after a while the euthanasia program was discontinued.

Some scholars have written that the ending of the euthanasia program illustrated the effectiveness of protest within the Nazi government. Recently, as more documents from that time have become available, scholars have reached a different conclusion. The euthanasia program for useless eaters, they believe, proved two things. People in small towns did not protest or block the taking of residents from asylums and clinics, and the pastors of the local churches did nothing to prevent the kidnapping of these people. When no one lifted a finger to stop these murders, the Nazis assumed they were safe. If citizens of a small town would not rally to save the lives of people they were related to, then they certainly would not care if the Nazis came later and took away the Jews.

The euthanasia program also gave the Nazis experience with the use of various gases, especially carbon monoxide. By the time Himmler declared that another way had to be found, the executioners had become expert in building structures for gassing.

At first, Jews were loaded into mobile gas vans, large trucks with sealed compartments, with the exhaust from the engine fed into the sealed compartment. At Lublin, Eichmann personally tested a closed truck. The prisoners screamed, and Eichmann noted later that it bothered him. When he peeped through a window in the cab and saw a hand grasping toward him for help, he said he wanted to get off. The driver assured him they were nearly finished. It is hard to know whether he was truly upset by the scene. If he was, he did not request a halt to the executions.

This is the interior of a gas chamber at Auschwitz.

The SS briefly expanded on the principle of carbon monoxide poisoning in large trucks. At Treblinka, the SS built special cabins that fed carbon monoxide from a Russian submarine engine into the sealed spaces. Eichmann was given a grand tour and shown the latest technological advances in how to murder Jews.

Though 1941 was indeed the year that atrocities began to take place on a large scale, the fulfillment of the Nazis' plans took another year or so. In July, 1941, Hermann Göring, Hitler's second-in-command, told Heydrich, who told Eichmann, that Hitler wanted him to prepare a general plan of the material and financial measures necessary for carrying out the Final Solution of the "Jewish question." The Göring memo has survived. At Göring's trial in Nuremberg after the war, the prosecution used it as hard evidence against him.

Oddly enough, Eichmann later claimed to a reporter that he wrote the memo that Göring gave to Heydrich. When he went to trial in 1961, his defense attorney said he was drunk when he bragged about his role in drafting the July 1941 letter. How deeply he was involved in top-level discussions will likely never be known. The rest of the paper trail has long since vanished.

The Wannsee Conference

There is certainly no question that Eichmann was involved in the infamous Wannsee Conference held in January 1942. It was at this meeting that decisions were made to go ahead with the systematic mass extermination of European Jews. Heydrich hosted the meeting. Eichmann acted as Heydrich's secretary, mailing invitations and coordinating arrangements. He claimed at his trial that he was a minor player at the conference. On the face of it, he would be right. Eichmann was the lowest-ranking Nazi in attendance.

Eichmann wrote Heydrich's opening address and kept the group focused as they discussed how best to carry out the details of the Final Solution of the "Jewish question." It appeared that no one even cared that Germany was fighting a war. Problems associated with troop movements or Allied bombings or keeping the soldiers fed and clothed were ignored. The whole focus of every officer and department was on the physical extermination of the Jews.

The Wannsee Conference did not change the overall methods of killing. By January 1942, the carbon monoxide chambers at Treblinka had been recognized as far superior to shooting. Cleanup was easier when the victims were gassed, and extracting anything of value from the corpses—hair, gold fillings in teeth—was easier.

What these officers discussed was how to make the killing more efficient, how to speed up the process, how to move the Jews more quickly from one place to another. The Wannsee Conference could have been a business meeting at any major corporation. The questions involved money and materials.

How can we spend less and kill more effectively? How can we keep supplies flowing at a steady rate so our factories are not idle? In this case, however, the factories produced dead people.

Once again, Eichmann found his niche. He was the perfect man for the job. He had proved that he was the most organized Nazi in the room. His efficiency astounded all who knew him. They knew they could count on him to keep the operation on track. And he knew the Jews.

The Wannsee Conference succeeded in unifying the Nazis around a common goal. For perhaps the first and last time in Nazi history, infighting was set aside as competitive military men agreed to work together. They put their resources at one another's disposal. Eichmann recalled later feeling both exuberant and exhausted as the relatively short meeting—it lasted only ninety minutes—came to a close. After everybody had lunch, Eichmann joined Müller and

Heydrich for drinks and a smoke around the fireplace. He was proud that they did not talk shop that afternoon, and only hung out together like the men in any other social club.

At his trial in 1961, Eichmann stated why the meeting held profound importance for him. He remembered thinking after everyone left, It's not just me. Everyone feels this way toward the Jews. Every single one of my superiors . . . they all want to take the lead in the Jewish question. What does it matter any more what I think? He described this as a "Pontius Pilate feeling," comparing himself to the Roman governor who allowed Christ's crucifixion. He believed that from that moment on there could never be any guilt pinned on him. He was only following orders.

5. Making the Trains Run on Time

Eichmann had convinced himself that he was not guilty of the deaths of the Jews because he had accepted the rationalizations of the Nazis and their new way of using language. Himmler also understood that if his SS men had to kill so many people, he would have to make them talk in terms that rationalized everything they did. "To have stuck it out and, apart from the exceptions caused by human weakness, to have remained decent, this is what makes us hard," Himmler had said.

The SS men selected for the *Einsatzgruppen* were taught to look at the murders as "awful things duty to my country demands." Murder became "granting a mercy death." The gas chambers at Treblinka, Auschwitz, and other extermination camps were renamed "The Charitable Foundations for Institutional Care." Eichmann embraced all this, finding in the euphemisms a way to still his conscience, or pretend. Eichmann's attorney in 1961, Dr. Servatius, inadvertently demonstrated how widespread the use of such language had become in Nazi Germany. During the trial, he casually referred to "medical matters" when speaking of the gas chambers. Horrified, the judges asked for clarification, and Dr. Servatius repeated his statement deliberately.

As Eichmann's work began, he would ask that the Jews being shipped in the cattle cars to their deaths not experience any unnecessary hardships. When an aide advised him that an entire trainload of Jews had arrived at one of the extermination camps dead from exposure to bitter cold, Eichmann ordered that on the next shipment the women and children should be allowed to ride in passenger cars, with only the men in the freight cars. He actually saw such acts as "mercy," and expected others to recognize that he had tried to reduce people's suffering on their way to the gas chambers.

Eichmann did in fact take a real interest in the workings of Auschwitz, which was his favorite concentration camp. Commandant Rudolph Höss, in charge of Auschwitz, tried to pin numerous offenses on Eichmann at his trial in Nuremberg. It is from Höss's testimony that historians came to believe that Eichmann personally selected Zyklon B as the most effective gas, once the top brass recognized that carbon monoxide simply killed too slowly.

Eichmann probably did attend the meeting at which Zyklon B was chosen. He did meet often with Commandant Höss to coordinate their activities. And he did witness at least part of the extermination process. He most certainly helped Höss design the layout of parts of the camp. But Eichmann's role really revolved around the most critical element of the whole plan—rounding up the Jews and shipping them to the death factories in an orderly fashion. Eichmann's job was

A member of the German SS supervises the deportation
of Jews at the Krakow ghetto in 1941 or 1942.

organizing transport. Murdering them fast
enough was Höss's headache, not his. There is
no record of Eichmann's response when Höss
once complained that Eichmann was sending
him more human freight than he could
possibly kill.

As a master of logistics, Eichmann worked
to set up a transportation grid that would
have seemed unfeasible to anyone else. One

of the first tasks required concentrating Jews in single locations. The idea of the Jewish ghetto had been around for a long time, but Eichmann modified it for his own purposes. In places like Lodz and Warsaw, he evacuated the non-Jewish residents of relatively small neighborhoods and packed in the Jewish population. He used his familiarity with Jewish leaders to set up Jewish councils in these ghettos. He knew how to work on their weaknesses, promising one day that a certain group would be spared if they complied with this or that order, or promising another day's delivery of a shipment of potatoes or carrots if they were compliant. He wanted lists of people's names and where they lived.

Eichmann was able to find corrupt Jews in some places, men who were willing to sell out their neighbors on the off chance that their own families would be saved. Almost without exception, however, once the rest of the Jews had been "relocated," these men and their families followed soon after. Occasionally,

Jews were forced to leave their homes and
live in the Warsaw ghetto in Poland.

Eichmann would choose a "favorite," someone who caught his fancy or whom he deemed cultured, and spare him. Two of these men later faced the wrath of the Jewish community, when their willingness to work with Eichmann was revealed. One was murdered and the other became an outcast.

One teenager who kept a diary in the Lodz ghetto wrote excitedly one day about the surprising generosity of the Nazi bosses. As food dwindled and people grew weaker from starvation, the Nazis came in and built a trolley system. The little train ran from one end of the ghetto to the other. The writer exclaimed that it made it so much easier to get to school and to the work he had to do, now that he did not have to slosh through mud. For a brief moment, the Jews in the Lodz ghetto believed that there was hope after all. The little trolley, however, was built so that the Nazis could move the weaker people to the train station, and from there to the extermination camp.

Eichmann's enthusiasm manifested itself in his search for Jews, which took him to all the occupied countries. Heydrich wanted Europe combed of Jews from "east to west." The highest priority was given to the extermination of those eastern European Jews who were less educated than their German or French counterparts.

A peculiar incident demonstrated how irrational Nazi logic could be. At a time when Eichmann was scouring Europe for more Jews to massacre, the Romanians had decided to outdo the Nazis. Without adequate rail connections to existing concentration camps, the Romanians built their own. In six months, the Romanians had wiped out 300,000 of their 850,000 Jews before Eichmann got involved in the process. The SS complained about the brutality of the Romanians, feeling that the murders should be carried out in a more civilized manner. They thought the excessive violence was out of order and wished to see it stopped.

Eichmann was alarmed at the reports and sent one of his top aides to assess the situation.

The aide returned and told him that the
Romanians were planning to send 110,000 Jews
across the Bug River into two forests on the
Russian side, where they would then liquidate
them. Eichmann summoned high-ranking
Nazis to his cause. The Romanians must not be
allowed to disturb his orderly efforts to get rid
of the Jews. In August 1941, Eichmann began
negotiations to remove 200,000 Jews from
Romania to the death camp in Lublin. To
prevent the butchery the SS so disliked, the
Romanians agreed that their Jews would be
evacuated by German troops. Before the new
plan could be carried out, however, the
Romanians "sold" their Jews. For $1,300 a
person, plus remaining assets, a Jew was
allowed to emigrate to Palestine, illegally.

Theresienstadt, a ghetto in Czechoslovakia,
was another oddity. Heydrich and Eichmann
saw it as their showplace for the world. Here
they would send Jews who were well known or
had important connections in places like the
United States, and here they would be treated

The Theresienstadt ghetto in Czechoslovakia. About 50,000 of its residents ended up at Auschwitz.

well. It was the only ghetto that was directly under Eichmann's command. About 50,000 of its residents ended up at Auschwitz. Theresienstadt is best remembered as the ghetto visited by the International Red Cross in 1945. The Nazis fooled Red Cross officials, who issued a positive report about the ghetto.

The ghettos, concentration camps, and railroads proved to be an effective system for delivering Jews to the extermination camps. In Lodz, Poland, 160,000 Jews lived in an area smaller than three square miles. Eichmann deliberately sent 20,000 more people to that ghetto, knowingly overloading it over the protests of the ghetto's district commander. More than 120,000 Jews in the Lodz ghetto died of starvation. Transport to the gas chambers was unnecessary, saving the Reich the expense.

A Change of Command

On May 29, 1942, Czech partisans assassinated Reinhardt Heydrich. The Nazis exacted vengeance for the assassination on the nearby Czech village of Lidice. They torched the town and killed all the men on the spot. Eichmann then arranged for the transportation of the 302 women and children to the death camps.

Heydrich's death caused a change in the chain of command. Eichmann's old friend Ernst Kaltenbrunner filled the position. Heydrich had proved a more effective advocate

Adolf Hitler and other Nazi officials
attend the funeral of Reinhardt Heydrich.

for Eichmann, who under Kaltenbrunner
suffered a series of minor setbacks. Among
other things, while he had been promoted to
the rank of lieutenant colonel, Eichmann never
achieved his goal of making general. Even at
his trial in 1961, when such regrets worked
against him, he bemoaned his unlucky fate, not
to have been promoted to the rank he believed
he deserved.

Eichmann continued in his role as the Jewish expert, but as the tide of the war turned, his section of the Gestapo lost some of its importance. Not because killing Jews was less important. If anything, Hitler stepped up the rates of execution the closer the Germans came to defeat. He almost seemed to have lost sight of the war he was fighting, concentrating solely on ridding Europe of all Jews at whatever cost to Germany and its soldiers. But Eichmann's role diminished because it became harder to kill Jews. With every Allied victory, access to his ghettos and rail connections was further cut off. Every Allied plane that bombed a train or railroad track destroyed his means of transporting Jews to the killing centers. And more SS units were needed to actually fight, making it difficult to find people to do the dirty work.

With a general's rank still in his mind's eye, Eichmann devised a new scheme to get rid of the Jews more quickly. He would offer to exchange one million Hungarian Jews for

10,000 trucks. Eichmann sent a Jewish leader named Joel Brand to central Turkey to attempt to negotiate the swap with the Allies. Brand was captured by the British and taken to Cairo, Egypt, where he was thoroughly interrogated. Finally, Lord Moyne, British resident minister in the Middle East, dismissed Brand with the statement, "What should I do with one million Jews?"

Having failed at this mission, Eichmann returned to his role as exterminator. Himmler ordered the shipments to the death camps stopped in 1944, not out of mercy, but because he wanted to start repairing the "damage" so that Allied troops would not uncover the extent of the massacres. He wanted to burn the bodies and fill in the mass graves, dismantle the extermination camps, and clean up as quickly as possible. Himmler saw this as the only way to avoid a death sentence after the war. Eichmann, for the first time in his life, purposely disobeyed orders. He rounded up another 50,000 Hungarian

Jews. With no trains available, he sent them on an eight-day death march.

Like the rest of the Nazi command, Eichmann spent the very last days of the war destroying as many documents as he could. He had been careful throughout his career to make sure that every order he gave could be traced to someone of higher rank, but in 1945 he attempted to purge his files of the

These are victims of the death march from Budapest to the Austrian border, November 8, 1944

smallest orders with his signature. He would have succeeded, but he had no control over the files of other Nazis, who were eager to prove their innocence at Eichmann's expense. He was not the only one who had practiced the art of covering his actions with letters from superiors.

Yet the single item that condemned him most clearly was not written on any scrap of paper. It was something he told a colleague, as the war was obviously lost, "I will leap into my grave laughing because the feeling that I have five million human beings on my conscience is for me a source of extraordinary satisfaction." When faced with these words quoted at the trial in Nuremberg, to the astonishment of the world, Eichmann did not deny them.

6. Escape, Capture, and Punishment

Germany surrendered on May 7, 1945. By Eichmann's own count, six million Jews had been killed in the extermination camps or by the *Einsatzgruppen*. But Eichmann escaped the attention of the Allied soldiers who rounded up Nazi offenders. An American unit did manage to capture him, but when he used the alias of SS Lieutenant Otto Eckmann or Corporal Adolf Barth, they believed him. Eichmann slipped away from the POW camp and disappeared. Neither Eckmann nor Eichmann sounded like important names to the Americans. No massive search ensued for the escaped prisoner.

At the International Nuremberg Tribunal after the war, when prominent Nazis were tried for their war crimes, Adolf Eichmann's name was mentioned several times. Commandant Höss of Auschwitz identified him as the Nazi bureaucrat in charge of the mass murder of the Jews, testimony supported by others. The international community added his name to the list of wanted criminals, yet it still took several more years before anyone understood how great his role had been.

As a result, Eichmann was able to disappear for many years. He worked as a lumberjack under the name of Otto Henninger. In 1950, five years after World War II ended, Eichmann made contact with the still-existing underground movement of SS veterans, known by the acronym ODESSA. They took him through Austria to Italy, where a Franciscan priest—fully aware of Adolf Eichmann's true identity—forged the documents necessary for Eichmann to emigrate to Argentina under the name of Ricardo Klement.

Eichmann's family joined him two years later, and his wife apparently never took on his new name. In fact, though Eichmann worked and lived under the Klement name, he almost flaunted his true identity. Argentina had been one of two havens for Nazi war criminals (the other was Egypt) that generally refused to extradite Nazis found to be living there.

These false identification papers were used by Eichmann while he was living in Argentina as Ricardo Klement.

When his fourth son was born in Argentina, the birth certificate had Eichmann as the child's family name. Veronika's Argentinian identity card showed her married name as Eichmann, even after she supposedly married Ricardo Klement.

Eichmann made a point of associating with former Nazis. And as the worldwide search for him gained in intensity, he seemed almost wistful for the fame that was passing him by. In 1955, a Dutch journalist and former SS man named Willem Sassen approached Eichmann about writing the story of his life. Eichmann not only consented but proofread the transcripts of the interview, noting corrections in the margins.

During the Sassen interview, Eichmann claimed personal responsibility for the most gruesome atrocities. He asserted that he formulated the Final Solution, that he chose Zyklon B as the poisonous gas for the death chambers, and that he worked with Göring on the July 1941 memo. Eichmann provided chilling details. He and Sassen congratulated themselves on a job well done, believing that they had a best-seller on their hands.

Despite the openness of Eichmann's lifestyle in Argentina, none of the dedicated Nazi hunters could find him. Perhaps no one could believe that such a powerful and wealthy

This is the house where Eichmann lived as Ricardo Klement in San Fernando, Argentina, in 1961.

man could live in a primitive brick house with no electricity and no running water in a poor suburb of Buenos Aires, working at a desk job for Mercedes Benz.

But Israeli agents did find him. They staked him out for months. Working undercover, they even asked him for directions, photographing him and his house to be sure they had the right man. In a daring kidnapping on May 11, 1960, they grabbed him in broad daylight on his way home from work. Eichmann actually signed a sworn statement saying that he was willing to stand trial. Hannah Arendt of the *New Yorker* noted a few years later that, as unbelievable as it seems, it is possible that Eichmann thought that if he was punished, German guilt would finally go away. He said this himself in a lengthy explanation to the court, and while no one accepted his words as true, Arendt wondered if he should be believed, for once.

The Trial

International reaction to the capture of Eichmann and his transportation to Israel was overwhelmingly negative. Even the United States ambassador to the United Nations, Henry Cabot Lodge, soundly denounced Israel's action before brokering an agreement that resulted in an official apology to Argentina by Israel. Argentina in turn finally dropped its request that Israel return Eichmann.

Israel organized a special police department, Bureau 06, made up of German-speaking police officers, to investigate the case against Eichmann, as well as to ensure that he did not escape. The officers of Bureau 06 undertook an extensive interview of Eichmann. The transcript of these tapes filled more than 3,500 pages.

Dr. Robert Servatius, a German national and a friend of Eichmann's stepbrother who had unsuccessfully represented several Nazis accused of medical experiments, volunteered to represent Eichmann. Almost a year passed between Eichmann's arrest and the start of the trial, a year that was filled with unprecedented international cooperation in the opening of closed archives from the Nazi period.

Since the government of Israel knew that the whole world would be watching the Eichmann trial, great care was taken to make it a show trial, yet one that would be just and fair. It would also be the first televised trial in history. The judges, Moshe Landau, Benyamin Halevi, and Itzhak Raveh, had reputations as serious, thoughtful adjudicators. All three were German Jews; all three had escaped Germany in 1933.

The Israelis built a bulletproof glass cage for Adolf Eichmann to sit in throughout the trial. It protected him from survivors of the death camps who might seek their own revenge, and it made it easier for the police to

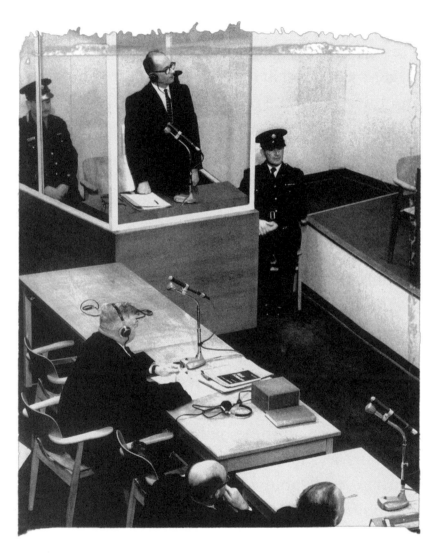

Adolf Eichmann stands in a bulletproof
glass enclosure in a Jerusalem court in
1961 as the judge reads the verdict.

ensure that the SS underground did not make a rescue attempt or slip him cyanide.

The trial quickly became a powerful emotional experience for the 750 observers allowed into the courtroom each day. In the more than fifteen years since the end of the war, the survivors of the extermination camps had kept quiet. Whereas German society had rebuilt and flaunted its wealth, survivors of Auschwitz and Treblinka, people who had lived through Sobibor and Bergen-Belsen, were ashamed to talk about what had happened to them. Now their stories would be told.

A few legal observers complained that Eichmann's trial was not the right place for these survivors to speak. Even the judges grew impatient with the prosecutor, Gideon Hausner, when yet another person spoke of the gas chambers, or wept as she described how her baby's skull had been crushed in front of her eyes. "What is the relevance of this with regards to Adolf Eichmann?" they asked.

Eichmann based his defense on two points. He had not personally killed a single person, and he was only following orders. Both points were ultimately rejected by the court. Commandant Höss may have, as Eichmann claimed, made the decision to use Zyklon B so he could murder 9,000 Jews a day instead of 2,000. But Höss's decision would have been meaningless if Eichmann had not delivered the human freight. The judges ruled that a cattle car could be a murder weapon in the same way the gas chamber was. Both made up parts of a lethal arsenal that had been unleashed for the sole purpose of slaughtering as many Jews as possible.

Adolf Eichmann's appeal was rejected by the Israeli Supreme Court. He was hanged at Ramleh Prison on May 31, 1962. At his request, his body was cremated and his ashes scattered at sea. His final words were: "After a while, gentlemen, we shall all meet again. Such is the fate of all men. Long live Germany, long live Argentina, long live

Austria. I shall not forget them. I greet my wife, my family, and friends. I had to obey the rules of war and my flag. I am ready."

Timeline

1906   March 19: Adolf Eichmann is born in Solingen, Germany.

1914   Eichmann's family moves to Linz, Austria.

1923–1932   Adolf Eichmann works at various jobs, including his father's mining company. The last six years, he is a traveling salesman for Vacuum Oil Company, an American-owned firm with a Jewish boss.

1932   April 1: Adolf Eichmann joins the Austrian National Socialist Party.

1933	January 30: Adolf Hitler is
appointed chancellor
of Germany.

April 1: Boycott of Jewish-owned
businesses in Nazi Germany.

1934	Eichmann, a corporal in the SS,
is stationed at the concentration
camp in Dachau.

September: Eichmann joins the
Sicherheitsdienst, or the SD, the
security service of the SS.

1937	Eichmann visits Palestine while
working on the "solution to the
Jewish problem."

1938	After Hitler annexes Austria in
March, Eichmann is transferred
to Vienna and put in charge of
the Central Office for
Jewish Emigration.

November 9–10: *Kristallnacht*,
"the night of broken glass,"
when Jewish businesses and
synagogues were destroyed
and burned.

1939

July 21: Eichmann opens Central Office for Jewish Emigration in Prague.

December: Reinhardt Heydrich appoints Eichmann head of the Gestapo Section IV B4 of the Reich Main Security Office. This promotion puts him in charge of the implementation of the Final Solution announced later.

1940

April 30: Lodz ghetto is formed.

July: Eichmann presents his Madagascar plan, proposing to relocate four million Jews to the island of Madagascar.

November 15: Warsaw ghetto is created.

1941

Eichmann begins aggressive supervision of the extermination of the Jewish people, visiting Auschwitz, watching a gassing by carbon monoxide poisoning, and observing mass executionscarried out by the *Einsatzgruppen.*

September 1: Jews are forced to wear yellow Star of David.

November 9: Eichmann is promoted to lieutenant colonel in the SS.

November 24: Theresienstadt ghetto is established and placed under Eichmann's direct control.

December 7: Japan attacks the United States at Pearl Harbor and and the United States enters the war.

1942

January 20: Eichmann organizes and acts as secretary for the Wannsee Conference, in which the Final Solution—a plan to exterminate all European Jews— is announced and put into motion

May: Reinhardt Heydrich is assassinated.

1943	January 30: Eichmann's old friend Ernst Kaltenbrunner succeeds Heydrich as Eichmann's commander.
1944	Germany occupies Hungary. Eichmann sets up commandos to implement the Final Solution. August: Eichmann reports to Himmler that approximately six million European Jews have been exterminated.
1945	May: The Nazis surrender and Eichmann is arrested. Using an assumed name, he escapes to northern Germany.
1950	Eichmann flees through Italy to Argentina under the name of Ricardo Klement.
1960	May 11: Israeli secret service captures Eichmann in Argentina and brings him to Jerusalem to stand trial.
1961	April 11 through August 14: The trial of Adolf Eichmann

in Jerusalem. The trial is the first ever shown on television.

1962   May 31: Shortly before midnight, Adolf Eichmann is executed by hanging.

Glossary

Allies
The Allies, or Allied Forces, in World War II were
made up of Great Britain, France, the United
States, and the Soviet Union.

Anschluss
The annexation of Austria by Germany in
March 1938.

Aryans
Germans and other people of Nordic or Germanic
heritage. The ideal Aryan was blond-haired and
blue-eyed.

Axis
The Axis Powers, centered around Germany,
included Italy and Japan.

boycott
An action in which one group of people refuse to

buy anything from another group of people
or to do business with them. In April 1933,
the Nazis called for a German boycott of all
Jewish stores.

Einsatzgruppen
The four elite killing squads of the SS that
followed the regular army as it swept across
Poland and Russia. They murdered Jews and all
political dissidents.

emigration
When people leave one country to go live in
another.

euthanasia
In Nazi Germany, so-called mercy killings, where
people with certain diseases or handicaps were
murdered "for their own good."

expulsion
Forced emigration, that is, when people are forced
against their wills to leave one country for
another.

extradite
To return a criminal who has fled the country
where he committed a crime back to that
country.

Gestapo
The Nazi secret police.

ghetto
A sealed-off part of a city where Jews were forced to live. The Nazis based the concept on the *shtetl* of eastern Europe, where Jews had to live inside walled cities and could go outside the walls only to work.

hyperinflation
An economic crisis in which money rapidly loses its value.

Lebensraum
Literally, "room to live." It was Hitler's primary war policy, justifying his invasions of places like Czechoslovakia and Poland.

Nuremberg Laws
The laws of September 1935 that legalized anti-Semitism and made it illegal for Germans to marry Jews and took away almost all the civil rights of Jews.

partisans
Members of small groups that tried to resist the Nazis by fighting behind the lines.

reparations
Payments made by the countries that lose wars to
the victors.

selection
At the extermination camps, the process of
choosing which prisoners would die
immediately in the gas chambers and which
would be used as slave labor.

swagger stick
A short, light stick used by military officers,
usually covered with leather, with metal tips
at each end.

Treaty of Versailles
The treaty that ended World War I and
forced Germany to pay the victors huge
reparations, which would help cripple the
German economy.

Yiddish
A German dialect spoken by German and eastern
European Jews.

Zionism
A movement of European Jews founded by
Theodor Herzl that called for a return of all Jews

to the land of Palestine and the establishment of a Jewish state.

Zyklon B

The poison gas used in the gas chambers of the Nazi extermination camps.

For More Information

Organizations

Holocaust Teacher Resource Center
P.O. Box 6153
Newport News, VA 23606-6153
e-mail: marknat@holocaust-trc.org
Web site: http://www.holocaust-trc.org

United States Holocaust Memorial Museum
100 Raoul Wallenberg Place SW
Washington, DC 20024-2126
(202) 488-0400
Web site: http://www.ushmm.org

Web Sites

Cybrary of the Holocaust
http://www.remember.org

Fortunoff Video Archive for Holocaust Testimonials
Yale University Library
http://www.library.yale.edu/testimonies

History Place: Holocaust Timeline/Adolf Eichmann
http://www.historyplace.com/worldwar2/
 holocaust/h-eichmann.htm

Holocaust Chronicle
http://www.holocaustchronicle.org

Holocaust History Project
http://www.holocaust-history.org

Holocaust Pictures Exhibition
http://www.fmv.ulg.ac.be/schmitz/holocaust.html

Holocaust/Shoah Page
http://www.mtsu.edu/~baustin/holo.html

Literature of the Holocaust
http://www.english.upenn.edu/~afilreis/Holocaus
 t/holhome.html

Nizkor Project
http://www.nizkor.org

Simon Wiesenthal Center
Museum of Tolerance Online
http://motlc.wiesenthal.org

Stephen Spielberg Jewish Film Archive
http://sites.huji.ac.il/jfa/

Teacher's Guide to the Holocaust
http://fcit.coedu.usf.edu/holocaust

Trial of Adolf Eichmann.
A companion Web site to the two-hour PBS
    documentary.
http://www.pbs.org/eichmann

Trial of German Major War Criminals
Includes the judgment of the International Tribunal.
http://www.nizkor.org/hweb/imt/tgmwc

Yad Vashem
Holocaust Martyrs and Heroes
    Remembrance Authority
http://www.yad-vashem.org

For Further Reading

Aharoni, Zvi, and Wilhelm Dietl. *Operation Eichmann: Pursuit and Capture.* Stuttgart: Deutsche Verlags-Anstalt GmbH, 1996. English edition: London: Cassell Military Paperbacks, 1999, translated by Helmut Bögler.

Frank, Anne. *Diary of a Young Girl: The Definitive Edition.* New York: Doubleday, 1995.

Matas, Carol. *Daniel's Story.* New York: Simon and Schuster, 1996.

———*Germans and Jews: A Photographic Diary.* Berlin: Nicolaische Verlagsbuchhandlung, 1996.

Serotta, Edward. *Out of the Shadows.* New York: Carol Publishing Group, 1991.

Sierakowiak, Dawid. *The Diary of Dawid Sierakowiak: Five Notebooks from the Lodz Ghetto.* London: Bloomsbury Publishing, 1996.

Spiegelman, Art. *Maus.* New York: Pantheon Books, 1991.

Wiesel, Elie. *Night.* New York: Bantam Books, 1982.

For Advanced Readers

Arendt, Hannah. *Eichmann in Jerusalem: A Report on the Banality of Evil.* New York: Penguin Books, 1965.

Schlant, Ernestine. *The Language of Silence: West German Literature and the Holocaust.* New York: Routledge, 1999. Schlant examines German literature from the end of World War II and discovers a disturbing trend: silence. Her book is indispensable for an in-depth understanding of the complexities of the German-Jewish issues that the Eichmann trial raised. Other sources include the news reports from the trial filed by reporters such as Homer Bigart and Lawrence Fellows for the *New York Times,* and the almost weekly updates in *Time* magazine, all available on microfilm in most libraries. Also see the excerpts of the Willem Sassen interview of Adolf Eichmann published by *Life* magazine in 1960.

Sibyll, Claus, and Jochen von Lang, eds. *Eichmann Interrogated: Transcripts from the Archives of the Israeli Police.* New York: Da Capo Press, 1999.

Index

Credits

About the Author

Ruth Sachs earned her undergraduate degrees in mathematics and German from Texas Christian University in Fort Worth, Texas. Sachs was challenged to consider the Holocaust by Frau Pieratt, her seventh-grade German teacher at Spring Branch Junior High School in Houston, who showed grainy black-and-white movies about her father, a scientist who had participated in the July 1944 assassination attempt on Adolf Hitler. While studying at the University of Augsburg on a Fulbright fellowship, Sachs traveled to Dachau with a student group. She has also written a novel about the White Rose resistance movement in Germany, and speaks to youth groups and synagogues about Holocaust issues.

Photo Credits

Cover photo © Archive Photo; p. 7 © AP Photo World Wide; pp. 10, 31, 41, 52, 82 © Archive Photo; pp. 13, 16, 18, 34, 37, 67 © CORBIS/Bettmann; p. 25 by Dr. John S. Kafka, courtesy of USHMM Photo Archives; p. 26 © KZ Gedenkstatte Dachau, courtesy of USHMM Photo Archives;

Series Design
Cynthia Williamson

Layout
Les Kanturek